Solar System

Welcome to This Book

Have you ever wondered why the Sun is hot? Or why the Moon looks the way it does? How about if there's life on other planets?

Scientists have asked these questions—and many others. They've used special tools to study the solar system. They've sent machines into space to gather information. And astronauts have risked their lives to learn even more.

What do scientists know about the many objects in space? What questions still need to be answered?

Target Words

These words will help you understand our solar system.

- **atmosphere:** the mixture of gases that surrounds a planet
  Earth's atmosphere is all around us.
- **gravity:** the force that attracts all objects to one another
  The Sun's gravity keeps our solar system together.
- **planet:** a large ball of rock or gas that circles the Sun
  There are nine planets in our solar system.

Reader Tips

Here's how to get the most out of this book.

- **Charts** As you read, be sure to look at each planet's chart. Charts can help you organize information. They can also make it easier to compare and contrast things. Check out Jupiter's chart on page 29. Look at its rotation. How does it compare to Earth's rotation (on page 16)?
- **Compare/Contrast** When you compare things, you see how they're alike. When you contrast them, you see how they're different. As you read about the planets in this book, try to compare and contrast them. This will help you remember and organize facts about them.

Solar System

Gregory Vogt

SCHOLASTIC INC.
New York   Toronto   London   Auckland   Sydney
Mexico City   New Delhi   Hong Kong   Buenos Aires

We are grateful to Francie Alexander, reading specialist, and
to Adele M. Brodkin, Ph.D., developmental psychologist, for their
contributions to the development of this series.

Our thanks also to our science consultant Ralph Winrich
of NASA's Glenn Research Center.

The images on the cover and title page are composite images, made up from
more than one photograph. They have been artificially colored.

Book design by Kay Petronio.

1 2 3 4 5 6 7 8 9 10   08   12 11 10 09 08 07 06 05 04 03

Contents

We live on a spinning, revolving **planet** called Earth. Earth belongs to a family of nine planets and more than ninety **moons**. At the center of this family is the Sun. The entire family is known as the **solar system**.

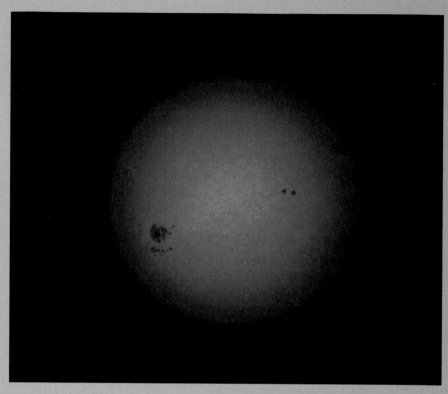

Cooler areas on the Sun appear as dark spots.

At night, we see thousands of **stars**. During the day, we see only one, the Sun. The Sun is a star. But the Sun looks much larger and brighter than the night stars. That's because it is millions of times closer to us than the stars we see at night.

THE SUN

The Sun is the center of the solar system. It is very big. If it were hollow, you could fit more than one million Earths inside the Sun.

Explosions of gas flare up from the Sun.

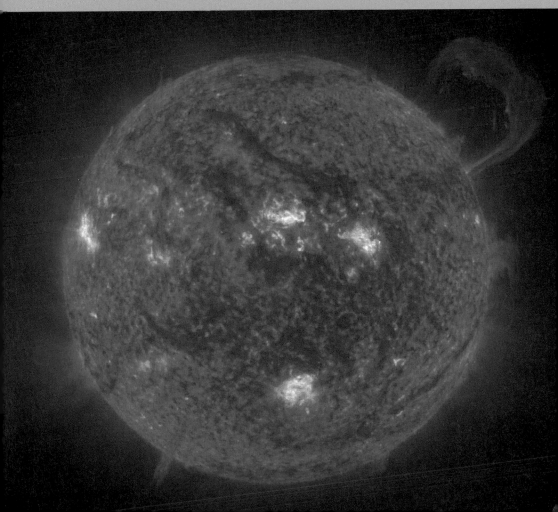

SUN	
Size Across	864,970 miles (1,392,000 kilometers)
Rotation (one complete spin)	24 to 34 days (The Sun's middle spins faster than its north and south poles)
Composition	Hydrogen, Helium
Temperature	Surface: 6,400°F (3,571°C) Center: 15,000,000°F (8,333,316°C)

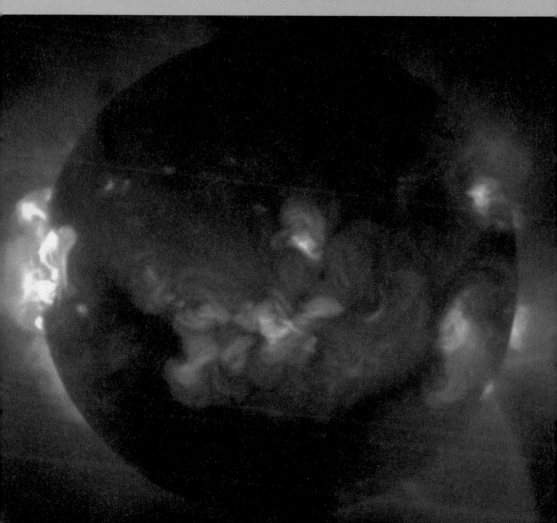

The Sun has **gravity**. Gravity is the force that attracts all objects to one another. The Sun's gravity pulls on the planets and moons. Gravity makes the planets and moons travel around the Sun. They follow paths called **orbits**. The Sun's gravity keeps the solar system together.

The Sun is very hot. It is made of gas. Deep inside, hydrogen gas is squeezed and heated to 15,000,000°F (8,333,316°C). It is turned into helium gas. When this happens, energy is released. It flows out from the Sun as light and heat. This is what we see and feel.

This is an X-ray view of the Sun.

MERCURY

Mercury is one of the smallest
planets. It is closest to the Sun. This
makes Mercury very hot. The side of
Mercury facing the Sun gets twice as
hot as a kitchen oven—800°F (427°C).
The dark side is three times colder
than Antarctica in winter—minus
297°F (minus 183°C).

Mercury is a rocky planet. It doesn't have air. The air around a planet is also called an **atmosphere** (**at**-muhss-fihr). Mercury doesn't have water, either.

Mercury's surface looks like the surface of Earth's moon. There are thousands of holes called craters. These craters were made when space rocks smashed into Mercury.

MERCURY	
Size Across	3,031 miles (4,880 kilometers)
Distance from the Sun	35,340,000 miles (56,872,662 kilometers)
Orbit Length (once around the Sun)	87.66 days
Rotation	58.66 days
Number of Moons	None
Number of Rings	None

VENUS

The second planet from the Sun is Venus. It is nearly as large as Earth. Venus is always covered with white clouds. The air around Venus is poisonous. The clouds are made of tiny drops of acid. The Sun's heat passes through the clouds. Then it gets trapped.

Maat Mons is a volcano on Venus. This image was created from data collected by the Magellan spacecraft.

Size Across	7,520 miles (12,102 kilometers)
Distance from the Sun	67,239,000 miles (108,207,000 kilometers)
Orbit Length (once around the Sun)	226.4 days
Rotation	243 days
Number of Moons	None
Number of Rings	None

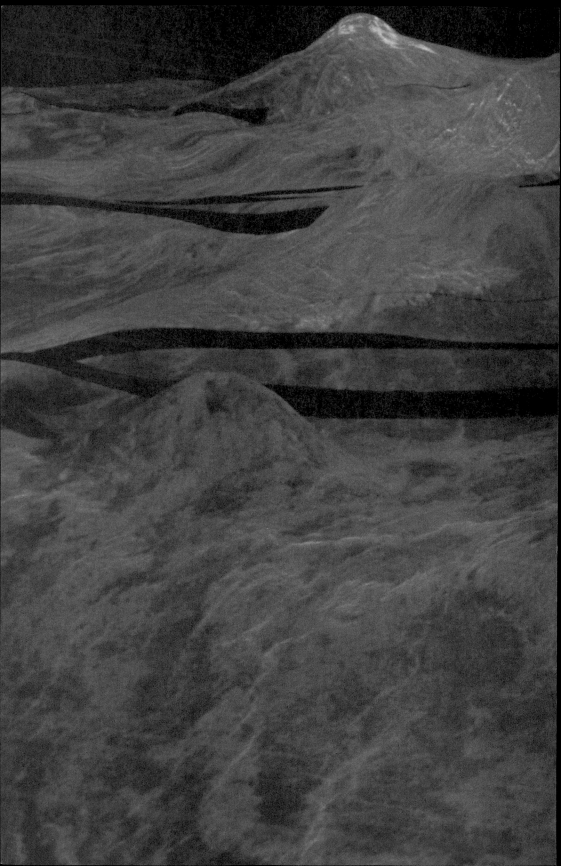

Trapped heat makes Venus the hottest planet. Metals like lead and zinc would melt on its surface.

Venus is made of rock that comes from volcanoes (vol-**kay**-nohz). The surface is covered with lava.

How do we know about Venus when we can't see its surface? **Astronomers** (uh-**stron**-uh-merz) study objects in space. They use spacecraft to study Venus. A spacecraft is a machine that travels to other planets. The *Magellan* spacecraft traveled to Venus. It sent radio waves through the clouds. Astronomers studied how the waves bounced back. This told them what the surface of Venus was like.

This view of Venus was also provided by Magellan.
The black spaces are gaps in the data.

EARTH

We live on the third planet from the Sun. Our home is mostly covered with water. The land is made of rock and soil. It has mountains, valleys, and plains. Some of the land is always covered with ice.

Living things are nearly everywhere.
Earth is home to millions of plants
and animals. They live on the land,
in the oceans, and in the air.

EARTH

Size Across	7,926 miles (12,756 kilometers)
Distance from the Sun	93,000,000 miles (149,000,000 kilometers)
Orbit Length (once around the Sun)	1 year
Rotation	24 hours
Number of Moons	1
Number of Rings	None

This is a volcanic eruption. The photograph was taken by astronauts on board a space shuttle.

Lots of air surrounds Earth. Winds blow white clouds. The clouds are made of water drops. The drops fall as rain or snow. Water runs across the land. And it wears the land away. Volcanoes spew out lava. And the lava makes new land. Earth is always changing.

EARTH'S MOON

One moon travels around Earth. The Moon is made of gray and black rock. The rock comes from volcanoes. Sunlight bouncing off the Moon makes it look white. The Moon's surface has millions of craters. One of them is called Copernicus. It is 58 miles (93 kilometers) wide.

Astronauts circling the Moon took this photograph of Earth.

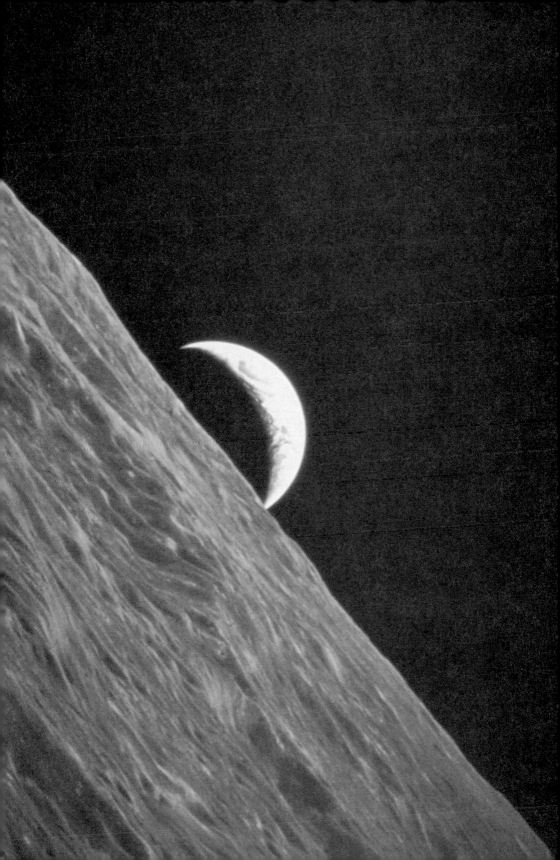

In 1969, astronauts landed on the Moon. They wore space suits full of air because the Moon has no atmosphere. They brought back moon rocks. Astronomers studied the rocks to learn how the Moon was formed.

This is astronaut Buzz Aldrin on the Moon.

In 1971, astronaut James Irwin worked on the Lunar Roving Vehicle.

Astronomers think the Moon was created billions of years ago. They think it happened during a collision. An object the size of Mars crashed into Earth. Earth was smaller then. Most of the object joined with Earth. This made Earth bigger. But a chunk of it flew off. This became the Moon. It has circled Earth ever since.

MARS

Mars is the fourth planet from the Sun. It is reddish in color. That's because it's covered with rust-colored rock and dust.

Mars has a giant canyon. It makes the Grand Canyon look tiny. The canyon on Mars is longer than the distance across the United States.

This image of Mars was taken by a space telescope.

MARS

Size Across	4,220 miles (6,794 kilometers)
Distance from the Sun	141,732,000 miles (228,089,300 kilometers)
Orbit Length (once around the Sun)	1.88 years
Rotation	24.62 hours
Number of Moons	Two
Number of Rings	None

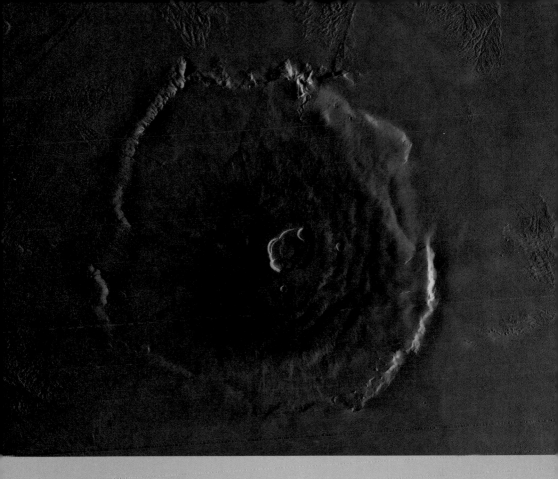

Mars also has very large volcanoes. One of them is three times higher than Mt. Everest.

Mars has a thin atmosphere. But there is not enough air for humans to breathe. If you went there, you would have to wear a space suit to stay alive.

This vehicle is called a rover. It was designed to explore the surface of Mars.

One of Jupiter's moons passes across its surface.

JUPITER

Jupiter is the fifth planet from the Sun. It is the first of four giant planets. It is made of gas. And it is eleven times wider than Earth.

Large clouds travel around Jupiter. The clouds are mostly orange and white. Winds blow the orange clouds one way. And they blow the white clouds the other way. This makes Jupiter look like it has stripes.

Jupiter also has a huge storm. It swirls like clouds in a hurricane (**hur**-uh-kane). The storm is twice the size of Earth.

Great Red Spot

Callisto

Ganymede

JUPITER

Size Across	88,849 miles (142,984 kilometers)
Distance from the Sun	483,879,000 miles (778,706,470 kilometers)
Orbit Length (once around the Sun)	11.86 years
Rotation	9.92 hours
Number of Moons	28 (possibly more)
Number of Rings	3

Astronomers have given this storm a name. It's called the Great Red Spot.

Jupiter also has many moons orbiting it. Two of them, Ganymede and Callisto, are larger than the planet Mercury. Another one has erupting volcanoes on it. And two others are covered with ice.

This image combines several photographs to show Jupiter and four of its moons.

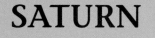

SATURN

Saturn is another giant planet made of gas. It is the sixth planet from the Sun. It has thousands of narrow rings circling it. The rings are made of rock, ice, and dust. They can be seen with telescopes from Earth. The other giant planets have rings, too. But they are much smaller. So they are harder to see.

Saturn's clouds are the color of butterscotch.

Saturn's rings are made up of thousands of narrow rings. The colors in this photograph were changed by a computer. That way, the rings are easier to see.

SATURN	
Size Across	74,900 miles (120,536 kilometers)
Distance from the Sun	888,615,000 miles (1,430,048,100 kilometers)
Orbit Length (once around the Sun)	29.46 years
Rotation	10.66 hours
Number of Moons	30 (possibly more)
Number of Rings	Thousands

An artist created this image of Saturn and some of its moons.

More than 30 moons orbit Saturn. Astronomers keep discovering more. One of them is very large. It is a few hundred miles wider than Mercury. It has strong gravity. The gravity holds an atmosphere of gas. Smaller moons do not have enough gravity to hold atmospheres. The gas surrounding them escapes into space.

URANUS

The third giant planet is Uranus. It is the seventh planet from the Sun. Uranus is four times larger than Earth. Chemicals in the air make it look green.

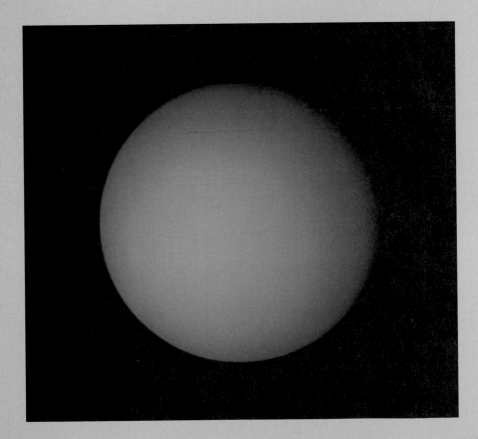

URANUS	
Size Across	31,022 miles (49,946 kilometers)
Distance from the Sun	1,787,274,000 miles (2,876,260,000 kilometers)
Orbit Length (once around the sun)	84.01 years
Rotation	17.24 hours
Number of Moons	21 (possibly more)
Number of Rings	11

Uranus is a sideways planet. It spins like all planets do. But it is tilted on its side. For half its orbit, Uranus's north pole points to the Sun. For the other half, the south pole points to the Sun.

Miranda is one of the moons of Uranus.

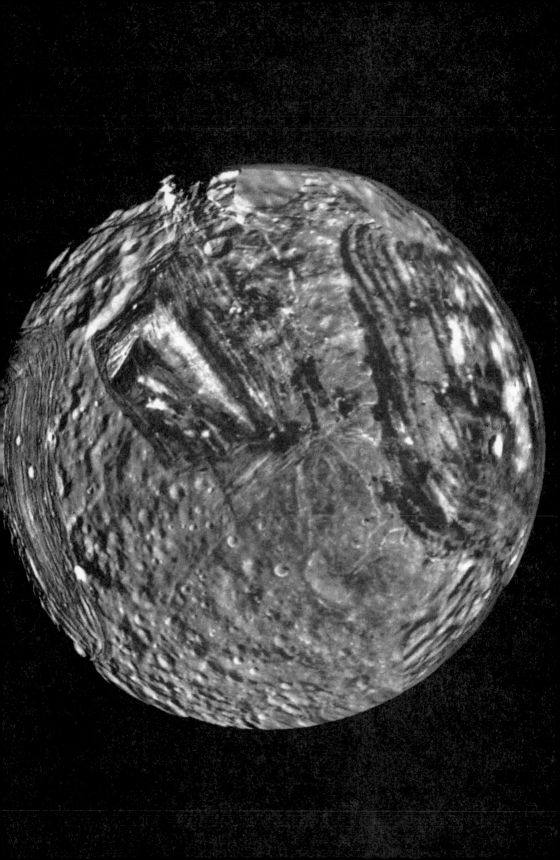

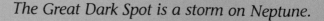

NEPTUNE

Neptune is the last giant planet. It is the eighth planet from the Sun. It is blue in color. And it is about as large as Uranus.

Neptune has storms like Jupiter's. But they are smaller. Sometimes, white clouds appear high in Neptune's air. Winds blow them around at speeds of over 1,200 miles per hour (1,931 kilometers per hour).

The Great Dark Spot is a storm on Neptune.

NEPTUNE	
Size Across	30,236 miles (48,680 kilometers)
Distance from the Sun	2,800,044,000 miles (4,506,110,800 kilometers)
Orbit Length (once around the Sun)	164.8 years
Rotation	16.11 hours
Number of Moons	8 (possibly more)
Number of Rings	6

———————— Great Dark Spot

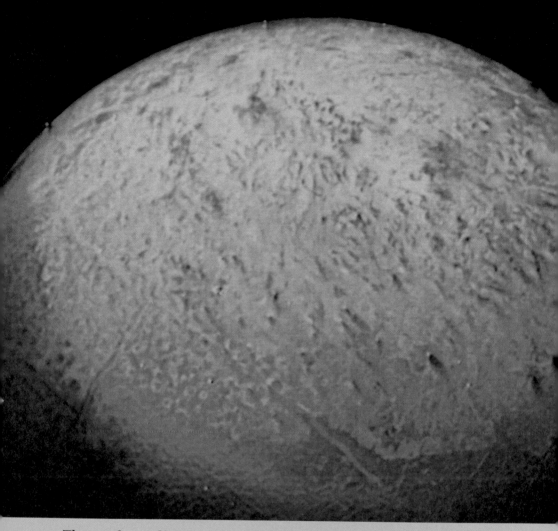

The surface of Triton looks like the outside of a cantaloupe melon.

Neptune has several moons. The biggest is Triton. Astronomers have noticed that Triton is getting closer to Neptune. Millions of years from now, Triton could smash into Neptune.

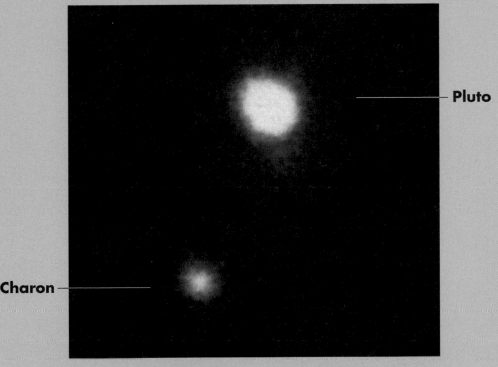

This is a photo of Pluto and its moon, Charon.
It was taken by a space telescope.

PLUTO

The smallest planet is Pluto. It is also
the last planet in the solar system.
Pluto is made of rock and ice. It has
just one moon. And the moon is half
the size of Pluto.

Astronomers don't know much about Pluto. That's because it's so far away. It would take a small spacecraft at least 15 years to get to Pluto. Pluto looks like a dark, fuzzy dot, even in the biggest telescopes. Sunlight on Pluto is 1,500 times dimmer than on Earth.

This drawing shows how a spacecraft used to travel to Pluto might look.

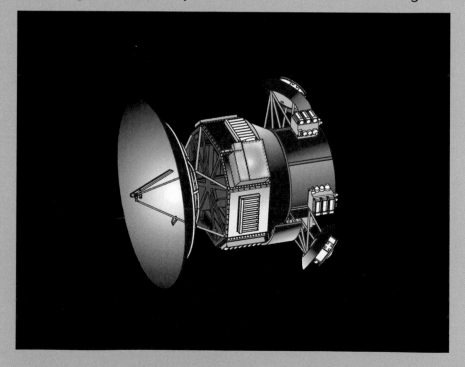

PLUTO	
Size Across	1,416 miles (2,280 kilometers)
Distance from the Sun	3,667,827,000 miles (5,902,633,900 kilometers)
Orbit Length (once around the Sun)	247.7 years
Rotation	153.3 hours
Number of Moons	1
Number of Rings	None

Some astronomers don't think Pluto is a planet. They think it's really just a large space rock called an **asteroid**. Other astronomers don't agree. Asteroids are shaped like giant potatoes. But Pluto is round like the other planets.

ASTEROIDS AND COMETS

There is still more to our solar system. Thousands of asteroids orbit the Sun. Some of them are hundreds of miles across. Others are the size of houses. Many asteroids orbit the Sun between Mars and Jupiter.

Far beyond Pluto are billions of large balls of ice called **comets**. Comets are usually a few miles wide. They orbit the Sun very slowly.

Sometimes, a comet gets bumped by another object in space and begins to fall toward the Sun. The Sun's heat starts melting the ice. A long white tail of gas streaks out for millions of miles. We can see the tail from Earth.

This is the comet Kohoutek.

EXPLORING SPACE

Astronomers study the solar system for many reasons. They use tools like telescopes to look at the planets. They send spacecraft to visit them.

One reason they do this is to find out where the solar system came from. Astronomers think the Sun's family started as a great cloud of gas and dust. Gravity caused the cloud to fall into itself. Most of the cloud became the Sun. Smaller clumps became planets, moons, asteroids, and comets.

Another reason astronomers study the solar system is to find out if we are alone. Is there life on other planets? None has been found yet. But someday, astronauts will travel to the planets. Mars will be first. Special cities may be built there for people to live. Then there really will be life on other planets. It will be us.

This is an artist's idea of what a base on Mars might look like.

Glossary

asteroid—a large piece of space rock

astronomers—scientists who study objects in outer space

atmosphere—the mixture of gases that surrounds a planet

comets—large ice balls that form long tails when they near the Sun

gravity—the force that attracts all objects to one another

moons—balls of rock or ice that circle planets

orbits—the paths followed by objects circling a planet or the Sun

planet—a large ball of rock or gas that circles the Sun

solar system—the family of the Sun, planets, asteroids, and comets

stars—huge balls of very hot gas

Index

Suggested Activity

Want to find out more about our solar system? A great place to check is the Internet site StarChild. StarChild is brought to you by the National Aeronautics and Space Administration (NASA). It is packed with useful information about and pictures of the Sun, planets, moons, stars, and more. You can also find interesting activities to try, and learn about being an astronaut and how space suits work. StarChild has links to other useful astronomy Internet sites. You can find StarChild at the following address:

http://starchild.gsfc.nasa.gov/docs/StarChild/StarChild.html